ONLY IN
CHURCH

VOLUME 1

*Hysterically Funny
Church Stories*

ONLY IN
CHURCH

VOLUME 1

Hysterically Funny Church Stories

compiled by Sheila Fredrickson

Published by Etcetera Publishing, LLC — Fort Worth, TX

ISBN 978-0-9818351-3-6
Printed in the United States of America
First Edition

Text Copyright 2012 by Sheila Fredrickson
Compilation, editing, layout and design by Sheila Fredrickson
Clip art by NVTech

Published by: Etcetera Publishing, LLC — Fort Worth, TX
www.EtceteraPublishing.com

Quantity discounts may be available on bulk purchases of this book for educational, business, or sales promotional use. Special books or book excerpts can also be created to fit specific needs.

For more information, please write to Etcetera Publishing, 6080 S. Hulen #360 - 174, Fort Worth, TX 76132 or email info@etceterapublishing.com.

www.OnlyInChurch.com

A Big "THaNK You"

to everyone who participated in my "experiment,"
contributing funny church stories for this first
edition of *Only In Church* through the website, via
email or by postal mail.

Reading your stories have made me laugh
again and again, and I hope sharing them
brought a smile to your face.

A very special "Thank You" to my husband and the
love of my life, Buddy, and my dear friend
Cindi Dawson, who provided constant
encouragement for this project.

Thanks, also, to my other family, both old and new,
who have shown me what a great blessing it is
to be loved *unconditionally*.

A Merry Heart doeth good Like a Medicine.

Proverbs 17:22

Table of Contents

Foreword 17

Author's Note 21

Wake Me When It's Over 23

Prayer Request 27

Missing in Action 28

At the Risk of Repeating 29

Let's Play Dress-Up! 30

Pulpit Supply 31

Gospel Who-dunnit 32

Amen! 33

Playing Along 34

Loose Teeth 35

Phone-y Business 38

Pew-fusion 39

Working Together 41

Accidents Happen 39

Can You Hear Me Now? 42

By Special Request.. 44

Pardon Me, But 46

Peas and Meat?... 47

The Streak 48

Happy Feet.. 49

Pass the Bread, Please 50

Children's Church.. 51

The Milkman 52

Bathroom Humor.. 53

Victory In Jesus 54

Misspoken Invite... 55

Look Again... 56

Pocket Change 57

Target Practice 58

Stay Tuned ... Updates To Come 60

Off On the Wrong Foot 60

Lose Something? 61

Hebrew Bible.. 62

Window Dressing...................................... 63

Surgical Mishap.. 64

Inky Walks the Aisle 65

Tall Tale.. 66

Hospital Bed.. 68

Wardrobe Malfunction.............................. 69

Littlest Angel 70

Be Still and Know 71

All Creatures Great & Small 72

Keyboard Chatter 73

"Sin" of Omission 74

Sparks 75

Give Me A "J"! 76

Still, Small Voice 77

About the Author 81

Book Order Form 99

ForeWord

Do you remember the funniest thing that ever happened to you in CHURCH?

And how much funnier it was because it WAS happening in church?

Maybe it happened to you, maybe to someone else. Not the normal funny stuff where someone drags toilet paper out of the restroom on their shoe, or gets their skirt tucked into the back of their underwear (although those are always good for a laugh).

No matter what kind of church you attend, a church is not the building, it's the PEOPLE. People do funny things even when they try NOT to!

Sometimes a funny church experience is even more hilarious because it's so hard to be quiet while you're laughing ... while trying to be serious. You're trying your best not to be disruptive and not to lose your composure, but it catches you off guard and you chuckle almost before you can stop yourself. You know what I'm talking about, don't you? You're chuckling about it right now. That chuckle probably reminded you of a good story. Do nice people laugh at things like this? Of course they do!

The Bible talks about laughter. You've probably seen these verses, which are among my favorites ...

Ecclesiastes 3:4 says,
"There is a time to weep, and a time to laugh,
a time to mourn, and a time to dance."

AND ...

Proverbs 17:22 says,
"A merry heart doeth good
like a medicine."

I hate medicine, but I DO like to laugh.

Funny church stories have become a favorite to me because things always seem funnier when you really want to laugh out loud ... but you can't!

Have you ever noticed how a good laugh makes you feel better? The world is a crazy place these days and sometimes you just want to crawl under a rock.

While there is a lot of serious stuff going on around, laughing has always helped me put things in perspective.

It is my hope these stories brighten your day, lighten your load just a little, and give you a needed chuckle in a hectic world.

— *Sheila Fredrickson*

Author's Note

Some of the stories in this book go back many years, to an earlier time when life was much simpler.

Things we used to laugh at may seem a little lame now, but at the time, they were the stuff memories are made of.

While compiling stories for this book, I realized that some of my best memories of growing up came from church services, events, and activities, and friends.

Every effort has been made to make this a "family friendly" book.

At the same time, a few stories were so funny that we could not leave them out despite their slant toward "real life." Our editorial committee had to make some difficult choices.

Many of the stories have been edited just a bit for length and content.

It is suggested that parents read the book first before sharing it with young readers, as a parent is always the best judge of what their child should read.

— *The Author*

Wake Me When It's Over

This is the story that started this little project ...

You know how when you get a new cell phone, sometimes it takes a little time to figure out all the features, even the basic ones? This was my first "smart phone," and I thought I knew how to mute the sound the first time I had it with me in church. I was pretty sure it wouldn't actually ring, and I was right about that, but *very wrong* about something else.

That's not funny in itself, but what happened because of it, in a church service, WAS.

I was looking at the Scripture passage in the Bible version I have in the phone, but it was a little warm in the building that day and I was literally falling asleep. (In fact, I'm not sure I didn't.) I thought, "Hey, if I could find something interesting to look at for a few minutes I would wake up. I really didn't want to fall asleep and start snoring right there in front of God and everybody. It would be pretty embarrassing to fall over on the lady sitting next to you, the one you just met who is visiting for the first time.

So ... I thought ... "Hmmm ... what could I read that might keep me awake until I can get focused on the sermon again?"

My mind started to really wander. (I've always had a little trouble staying focused, but this went way beyond that.)

As the pastor got deeper into his message, I was *far* away, and realized I wasn't limited in what I could look at, because my new phone had INTERNET!

All this happened in the space of probably about 2 or 3 minutes. By this time, I was not paying attention at all!

I realized I had access to a movie preview service on my phone, so I looked at that for a few minutes, and then I thought, "I wonder if classic movies have previews on here?"

I searched for "The Sound of Music," and found it ... then I searched for "Fiddler on the Roof," and found it, too!

All this time, I had not heard a sound out of my phone. Suddenly, that changed when the sound of "If I Were A Rich Man" came blasting out.

If I had been sleepy up until now, suddenly I was wide awake as I tried to figure out how to turn it OFF.

Whatever I did, it worked.

Had anyone heard? I hope not. Nobody said a word.

All anyone would have had to do was glance my direction, and they would probably have seen the panic-stricken look on my face!

Next time I need to wake up in church, I will find something to read ... something without sound!

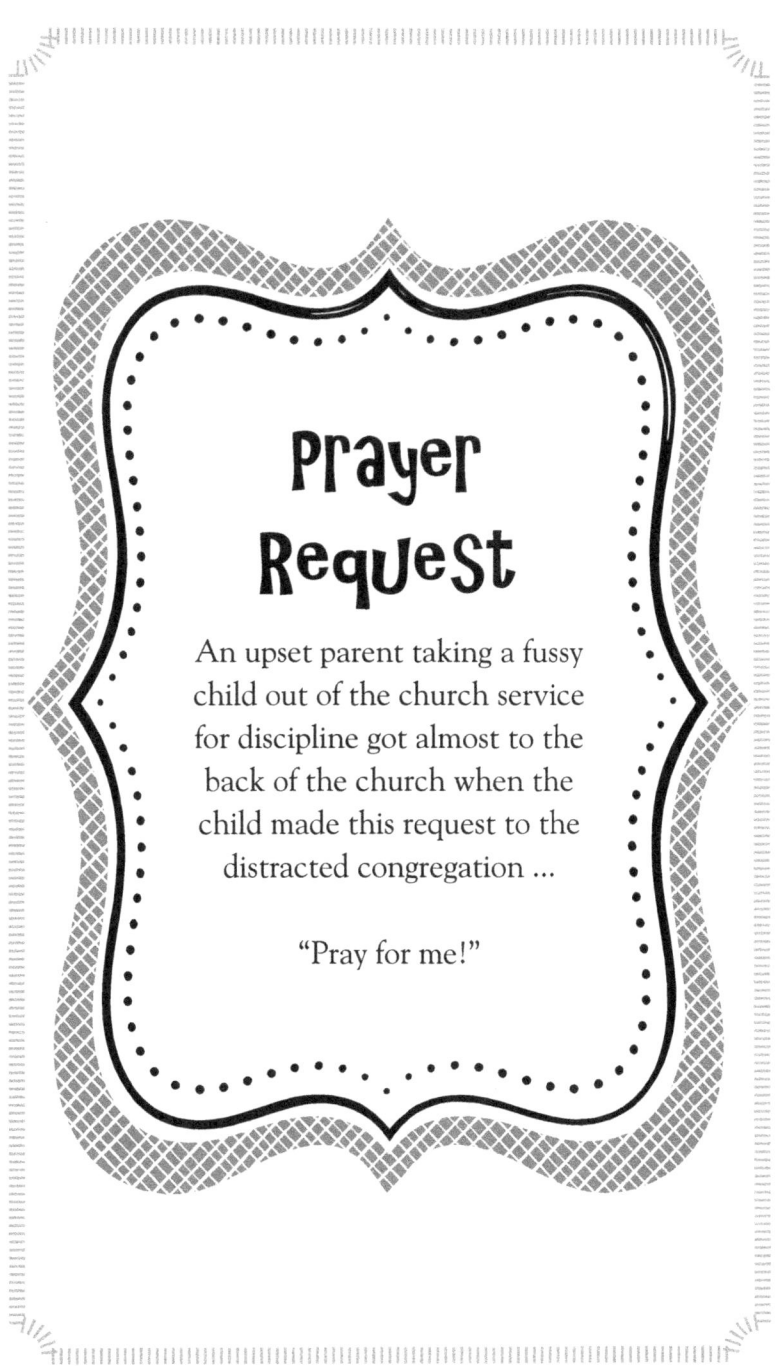

Prayer
Request

An upset parent taking a fussy
child out of the church service
for discipline got almost to the
back of the church when the
child made this request to the
distracted congregation ...

"Pray for me!"

Missing In Action

I am the organist at my parish. When my daughter was little (about age 5), the sitter cancelled the morning I was to play for a funeral. So ... I took her with me.

There is a small room off the choir balcony. I set her up with blanket, pillow, and a few toys with the promise of a toy if she was really good.

After the prelude and opening hymn, I went to check on her. She was gone!

I tiptoed down to the church foyer — no luck! I then continued to look for her during the homily. I was getting a little panicky by this time. Then as I turned the corner one more time, I spied her foot under the organ bench.

At some time while I was playing, she had crawled under the bench and fallen asleep! Although I was quiet during the search — I am sure it was quite a scene to watch the balcony from the sanctuary!

25,000 ÷ 3 = ?

At tHe RiSK oF Repeating

My mom and dad were sitting in church one Sunday morning. The pastor was trying to explain some statistics by stating that women use about 25,000 words a day, while men use only 5,000.

My 83-year-old mom immediately stood up right in the middle of the sermon and said, "Do you know why women use 25,000 words a day?"

The pastor said, "Well, no, I don't. Why don't you tell us?"

She said, "Because women have to repeat everything they say three times before it's heard."

My dad, sitting next to her, looked up at her and with a puzzled look on his face said, "Huh?"

Order was finally restored after several minutes of laughter.

Let's Play Dress-Up!

My grandchild always attends church with me and is on the church property every day because I work there. She knows everyone she sees and is well-accepted there.

We were in church one Sunday (she was almost 3 at the time) as she watched the pastor walk up to the altar.

Now the church is quiet and we are in the back of the church when she blurted out loudly, "Why is my pastor wearing a dress?"

The whole church laughed as they turned around to see who said it. Our pastor turned to face the congregation with a smile on his face, and didn't miss a beat with his introductions.

I was ready to crawl under the pew as I tried to explain to my granddaughter that he's not wearing a dress, it's a robe. Her reply was, "Well, it looks like a dress!"

PULPit Supply

While preaching one of my first sermons ever, filling in for the pastor, a young lady who had married a year earlier and moved away was in our small congregation that day.

Even though I was very nervous, I thought I should acknowledge her being there so I said, "It's so good to see Amy and her husband here with us today."

She promptly replied, "This is not my husband."

My mind immediately went into overdrive as I thought of various reasons why she would come to church with some man besides her husband.

Since none of those scenarios seemed like a good idea I just said, "Oh, OK," and went on with my sermon.

It turns out everyone but me knew the gentleman seated next to her was her brother, a young man I too had met on several occasions several years before. (I thought he looked familiar!)

Everyone agreed that I set a record for the longest blush of embarrassment they had ever seen.

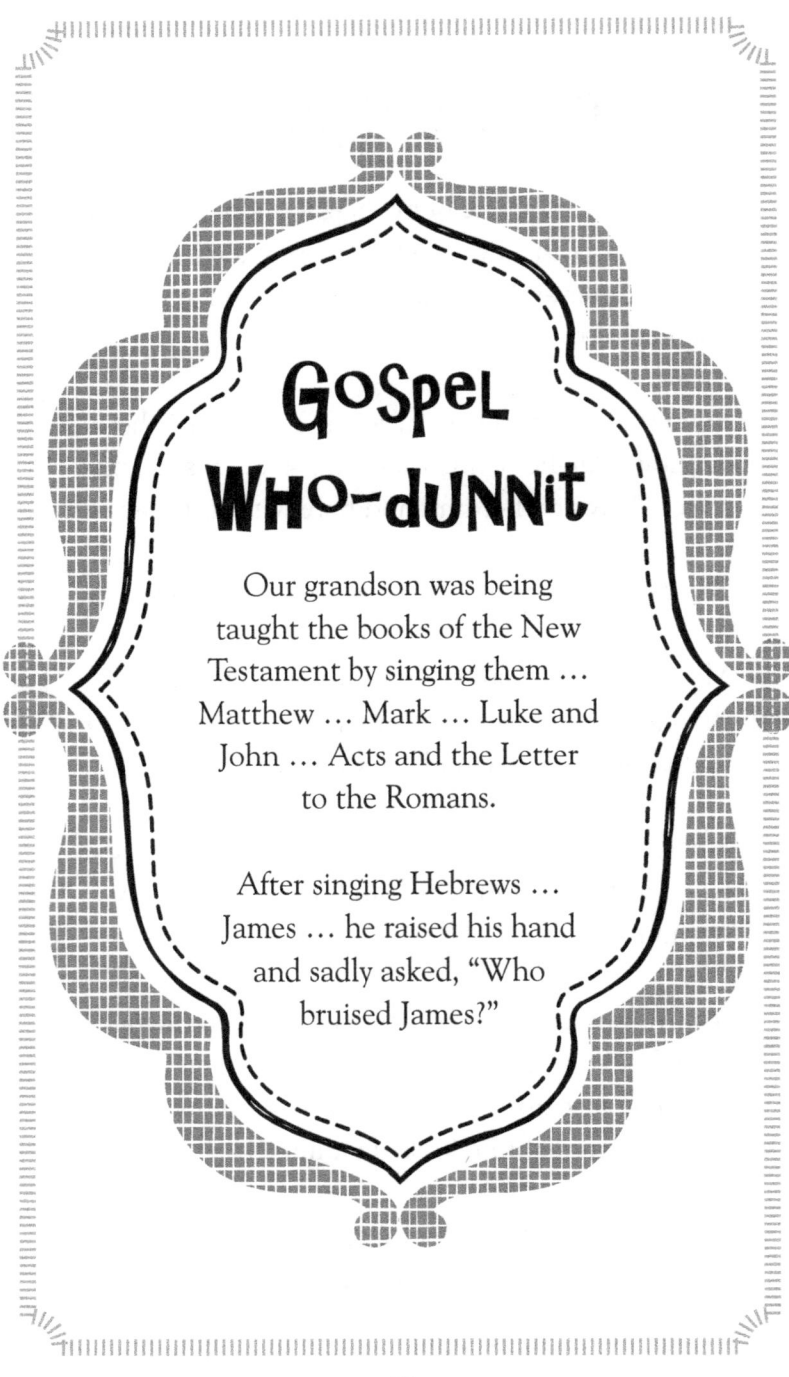

GoSpel
WHo-dUNNit

Our grandson was being
taught the books of the New
Testament by singing them ...
Matthew ... Mark ... Luke and
John ... Acts and the Letter
to the Romans.

After singing Hebrews ...
James ... he raised his hand
and sadly asked, "Who
bruised James?"

AMeN!

It's Easter Sunday. Our 21-month-old-daughter is sitting on my wife's lap during church.

The pastor was a real "fire and brimstone" type preacher, and he had the entire congregation going during his sermon.

He was walking up and down the aisle, and people all around were shouting "AMEN!", "YES!" or "You tell it, Pastor!"

And throughout the whole time, our daughter sat enraptured on my wife's lap. She had the biggest smile on her face, and she loved watching all these people shout "AMEN!"

Finally, the pastor said two words and paused: "In conclusion ..."

Immediately, our daughter shouted "AMEN!" The entire congregation exploded in laughter and my wife turned as red as her dress.

We found a new church after that.

PLAYiNG ALONG

One of the ministers was making a childrens'
announcement about the upcoming activities in our
Vacation Bible School week.

He was supposed to say that one activity was
working with play dough to make different designs.

"Well," he said " ...
and the children will
be working with 'play
boy' to create different
things."

There was a moment
of silence over the
congregation, then just
a loud roar of laughter.

The minister got a funny look on his face, and did
not realize what he had just said.

Try to deliver a sermon after that!

Loose Teeth

My mother would probably cringe with embarrassment if she knew I was writing this story about the funniest thing that ever happened to me in church ... or should I say, to her? Thankfully for her though, I do not need to submit my name, or hers, or the poor pastor's mother who was also involved.

This took place in the early eighties. My mother had just gotten a set of false teeth, and she was experiencing a few difficulties with them.

One of her complaints was that they would always come loose.

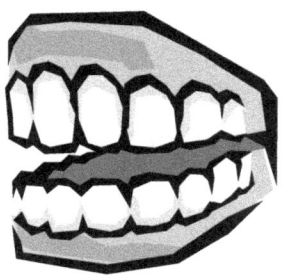

Well, one Sunday, as we were all sitting in church, my mother began to sneeze. Once, then twice in a row. She opened her purse and was rooting inside for a tissue, when again, she sneezed twice in a row.

Between looking for the tissue, and trying to thank those around her for the "God bless you's" she was getting, yet another sneeze came. Suddenly out of the corner of my eye, I saw something fly quickly in front of her. The object projected out of her mouth, and hit the back of the head of the poor woman who was sitting right in front of her. The woman felt it, and turned around to see what had struck her head, just as my mother realized that her teeth had flown out of her mouth. Not only had they struck the pastor's mother in the head, but they also decided to fall in the collar of the dress she had been wearing. The poor lady didn't realize what had struck her yet, or that my mother was now horrified to see her teeth resting on the back of the woman's collar. My mother was red-faced as she reached out to retrieve her teeth from the woman's clothes, and muttered an apology to her. The poor woman looked shocked at first, but then a soft chuckle soon turned into an outrageous laugh, making her have a hard time catching her breath.

Of course, me being a young 13-year-old girl, I was absolutely horrified, because now everyone was looking at us and wondering what was so funny. Teenage girls become very embarrassed over things like that, so I did the only thing I could think of, which was to whisper at my mother, who was now laughing as well, to hurry up and put her teeth back into her mouth so people wouldn't see. That is when she realized she was being seen without her teeth and quickly put them back into her mouth, now with many people watching her, including the pastor, who had by this time paused his sermon to see what the cause of the disturbance was.

He made some comment, which I can't recall exactly, but remember that it was pretty funny, and then the sermon continued on as usual.

For the next few weeks, my mother was the source of many loving, yet teasing jokes ... and when someone would sneeze at church, instead of, "God bless you!" it became typical to hear comments such as, "Uh-oh, everyone duck!"

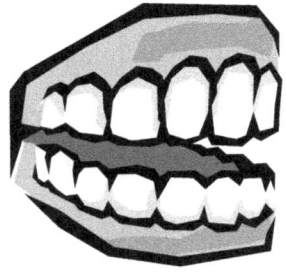

PHONe-y BUSiNeSS

The funniest thing I can remember in our church was the morning that our Minister of Education & Music stepped up to the pulpit to begin the next worship set when his cell phone rang.

The entire congregation just lost it when we heard him say, "Well, Dad, I'm in church now. Can I call you later?"

PeW-FuSioN

Our nephew was visiting us at our home.

When Sunday came we took him to church with us. Everything went well until it was time for communion.

The church was not full because in the summer, attendance is always lower. We got up and received communion. My nephew was leading us back to our pew. When we got back to the pew and knelt down — we realized we had gone back to the wrong pew.

That wouldn't have been so bad, except we were in the front so every single person in our section ended up in the wrong pew. When we realized what had happened, we looked back and people were passing their purses, rosaries, jackets etc. back to the people behind them because everyone was in the wrong pew. Of course we stared giggling to the point that our shoulders were shaking. It was very hard to compose ourselves.

When Mass was over people came up to us and made the comment, "We really are sheep ... we follow so easily."

Working Together

Our lesson that Sunday was about Josiah and the restoring of the Temple, and everything we did that Sunday had to do with cleaning and building. We used real paintbrushes with the tempera paint, had tool kits and brooms in center time, and "built" sandwiches from bread, cheese and bologna.

During worship time, we sang "When We All Work Together." The words go like this: "When we all work together, together, together ... When we all work together, how happy we'll be!"

After singing a few times, we asked the children to suggest specific examples of work — an object or an action. We started out with "broom": "When we all sweep together, together, together ... When we all sweep together, how happy we'll be!" Then a child wanted to "saw": When we all saw together, together, together ... When we all saw together, how happy we'll be!" The next little girl chose "hammer." And then a kindergarten boy called out, "screwdriver." Sing it yourself, and you'll see why we still count this among the funniest moments ever in church.

Accidents Happen

When I was a baby, our church had hard wooden pews. I was not yet potty-trained.

One of our elderly and quite sophisticated deacons was sitting at the end of the pew I was sleeping on, next to my mom.

The pew wasn't level because when I relieved myself in my diaperless bottom, it proceeded to run down the pew, and soak into his light-colored and expensive suit pants.

This would not have been a big deal if he hadn't been napping too, but when he felt the warm liquid, he jumped up and exited down the center aisle!

I'm afraid the pastor, who was my uncle, was the only one in the church who knew it was me and not the elderly deacon who had the accident.

I think my mom later confessed it to him, and he kept the secret to his grave.

Can You Hear Me Now?

Our church upgraded the sound system and added a hearing-impaired system. We decided to give our members and guests the option to either check out the individual wireless receivers or to purchase one of their own to avoid the process of signing them out every service.

Several of our members purchased their own personal receiver. On the Monday after our first attempt to use the new system I was visited in my office by one of our elderly ladies who had spent the money to purchase her own personal receiver.

She was somewhat upset, so I inquired about what had her so frustrated. She said that her receiver did not work. I told her that each receiver had to be tuned to our system's frequency and perhaps her unit did not get the exact setting.

I offered to check it out while she waited. I took it into the worship center, powered up the sound system, played a CD and began to listen through her receiver. Loud and clear came the signal.

I walked all through the seating area and had no problems with the unit. I went back to the office and asked her exactly where she was sitting so I could test it once more from her seat.

That is when the scene became increasingly funny to the staff, but very frustrating to her. She said very matter-of-factly, "I was in my recliner in my living room at home." I could hardly contain my smile

as I replied that these units only worked inside the worship center.

With great frustration she replied, "You mean we spent all that money on this system and I can't even enjoy the service from my own living room?"

I responded with much grace, trying to explain that the purpose of the system was to help those who attended with hearing problems, not to broadcast our worship service all over the community.

Disappointed and dejected, she meekly requested her money back for the receiver that she would no longer need, as she could hear just fine when she came to church.

By Special Request

When my son was five years old and in kindergarten, my husband was the music director and I was the pianist at church.

My mother would sit with my son while we played and led music before the sermon. One night we had "Request Night" for hymns. My husband had already said that if anyone called out a number of a song that he didn't know, they would have to come up and lead it.

My son raised his hand between every song, indicating that he wanted to request a song. Finally he was allowed to call out a number. He proudly stated he wanted to sing #250 in the hymn book.

Everyone turned to #250 but no one knew the song, including me. My husband squirmed a bit and I began to play the introduction to the song and finally the music was stopped and everyone laughed when my mother looked over my son's shoulder to see that he meant to call out #205, which everyone knew.

My mom said out loud, "It's #205, not #250!" When the laughter died down, she said, "Oh give him a break, he's only five years old!"

That was it and we all lost control of ourselves laughing so much we had to stop the requests and just go straight into the sermon.

Pardon Me, But ...

My husband and I were serving communion one Sunday, and as one lady got up from the communion rail I noticed something around her feet. She begin shuffling her feet as if she couldn't walk. I looked at her feet and lo and behold, her slip had fallen to her feet when she stood up!

It was the funniest thing I had ever seen in my life and my husband and I didn't dare look at each other or we would have started laughing uncontrollably in front of the whole church.

What did she do, but flip her slip up with her foot and stick it under her arm before going back to her seat. My husband and I held our composure until we got to the back of the church after the service, and then begin laughing so hard we just sat there and laughed for about twenty minutes, tears rolling down our faces.

The lady now says she never attends church on communion Sunday without pinning her slip to her girdle!

To this day it is still the funniest thing I have EVER seen.

Peas and Meat?

While teaching a Sunday school class of 3-year-olds, the Sunday lesson that rolled around was David and Goliath.

We acted out the events with one little boy playing the part of David.

As he approached Goliath he said, "Do you want peas and meat?"

The children finished their reenactment with the Philistines running for the hills.

I had to ask the little boy what he said to Goliath.

He got back in his fighting stance and said again, "Do you want peas and meat?"

After some conversation back and forth and some frustration on his part, it finally came to me that he was actually asking, "Do you want a piece of me?"

The Streak

Back in the days when people "streaked," i.e. ran around in a crowd without clothes, my husband Larry was a pastor.

During a sermon one Sunday morning after attending an exciting boys' basketball game the night before, he used part of the game as an illustration.

He said, "And you should have seen "Joe" streaking down the court last night."

Needless to say, everybody laughed in church that day.

Happy Feet

As the Minister of Music of a small Baptist church in a tiny Texas town, my wife and I often arrived early at church on Sunday morning to practice the special music before anyone else arrived.

Our 2-year-old daughter enjoyed playing in the church sanctuary while we rehearsed.

One Sunday morning while listening to us rehearse, she started dancing to the music.

In addition to dancing, she pulled her dress up over her head while she moved.

She was obviously having a great time and we laughed, that is until one of the older deacons walked in with his wife.

They didn't say a thing, but the glares we got were unforgettable.

We got a good laugh later when no one was watching, and although it has now been almost thirty years, it still brings a chuckle.

PaSS tHe Bread, PLeaSe ...

I was seated in the choir loft on a Sunday when The Lord's Supper (Baptist version of communion) was served during a worship service.

The "bread" I picked up was *tiny*, no more than a shard. It was not long before it slipped out of my hand and fell on the floor.

When I realized it was gone, I tried to contain my laughter but tears began to roll down my cheeks and I was helpless to stop them.

After the service, several people told me they had noticed how moved I was during the service.

If they had only known!

CHiLdreNS' CHUrCH

I play the guitar and my children would sing along
with me at home. We sang many songs together,
with one of their favorites being "Jesus Loves Me."

When my son was about 3 years old (he is now 33),
he would sit in the front row with other little ones.

This particular Sunday I happened to be doing the
special music. I was singing a song I had just written
and was excited to share the song God had given
me.

As I started playing the introduction, being very
serious because of the message the song would bring,
my young son stood up and started singing at the
top of his lungs "Old MacDonald had a farm, E I E
I O."

Needless to say, the mood changed and it took me
several minutes to regain my composure to try again.

The best part of the story is, I have it on "tape."

The Milkman

My niece was born with beautiful auburn hair ... the kind that makes others green with envy. Naturally thick and the perfect touch of red — not too brassy.

From the time she was a little girl everyone would stop my brother and comment on how beautiful that child's hair is. Neither my brother or his wife have red hair, nor does the majority of our family.

As genetics would play out later on, my second brother and then myself would each be blessed with a red-haired child, but my niece was the first so the question was often raised, "Where did she get her red hair?"

Well ... one Sunday morning in the foyer of the church during "meet and greet" time, the pastor, our lifelong family pastor, reaches down and takes her little hand to greet her and says, "Honey, you have the prettiest hair ... where did you get that beautiful red hair?" to which she answered, "My mommy says the milkman did it!"

Oh ... was there some explaining to do!

Bathroom Humor

One Sunday morning as the young minister led the congregation to turn to the book of the Bible from which he would be reading at the beginning of his sermon, he inadvertently said, "Turn to the book of John."

After a few seconds his congregation heard him say softly, 'I'm in the wrong John!' "

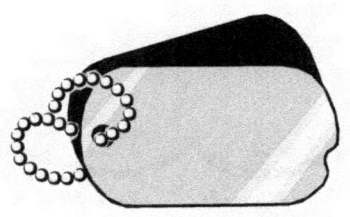

Victory in Jesus

My youngest son developed challenges with his hearing as a child, and he also had difficulties paying attention during worship.

Therefore, it shouldn't have come as a shock to us when we heard him deliver his own lyrics to "Victory in Jesus" as "Oh, vickery in Jesus, my Savior forever. He socked me and bopped me ... etc."

Additionally, "Jesus is Lord" became "Jesus is bored ..."

Thanks to God his medical issues have been dealt with satisfactorily and he is a productive active member of our Armed Forces, but the memories always bring a smile to my face even years later.

MiSSpoKeN INVite

At the end of my message, I invited those who were new to meet me in the lobby to say "Hi!"

I fumbled through my words and said, "If you're NUDE today, I would love to meet you in the lobby."

I realized what I had said, but instead of just moving forward I tried to explain myself and said, "Did I just say NUDE?"

The more I tried to get out of it, the worse it got, and I felt as though I was digging a hole.

No one showed up, but I got some great feedback from my staff!

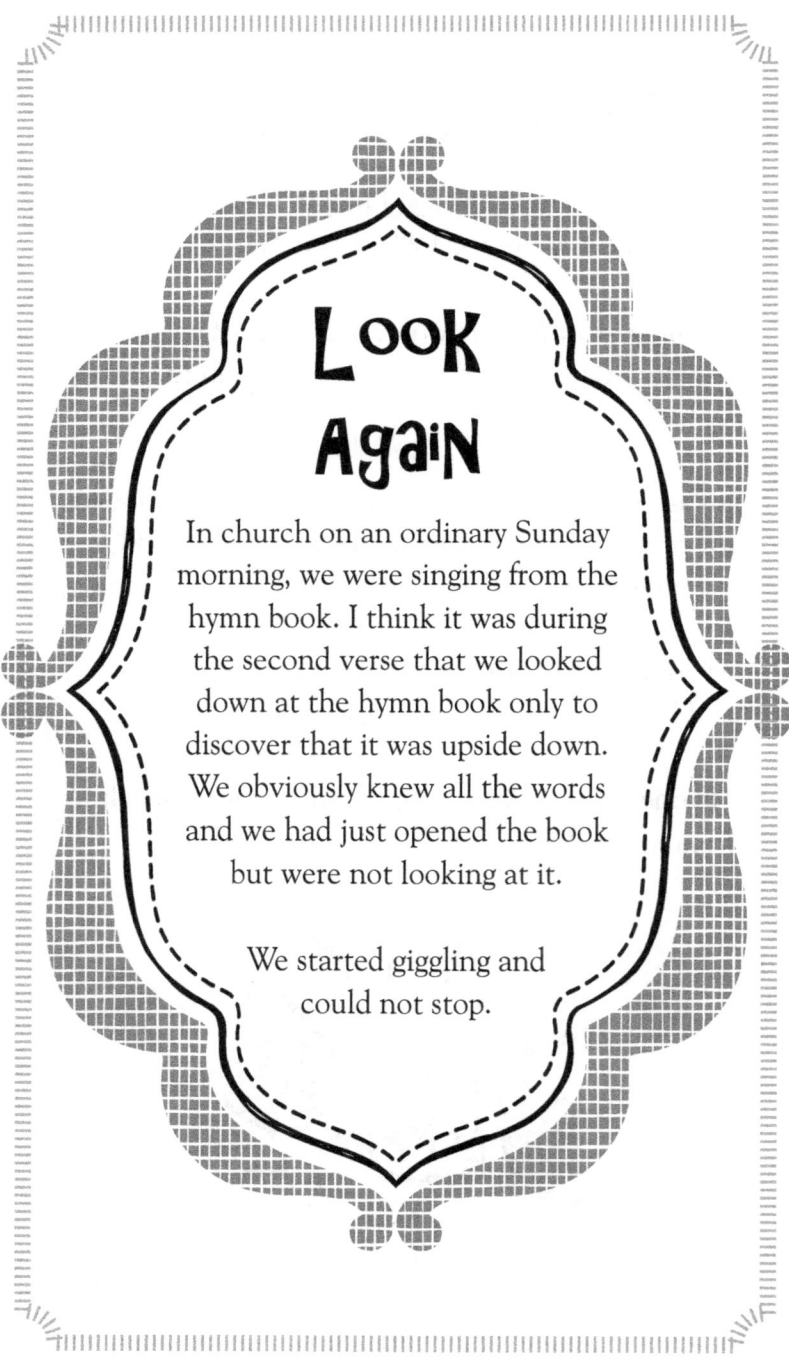

Look Again

In church on an ordinary Sunday morning, we were singing from the hymn book. I think it was during the second verse that we looked down at the hymn book only to discover that it was upside down. We obviously knew all the words and we had just opened the book but were not looking at it.

We started giggling and could not stop.

Pocket Change

As a youth, my pastor told me how he often used throat lozenges while preaching.

When beginning to speak he would reach into his suit pocket, grab a loose lozenge, and put it in his mouth with no one noticing.

On one occasion, he could not figure out why it was not melting in his mouth.

At the end of the service, he took it out and discovered it was not a lozenge ... it was a button!

Target Practice

I was giving a sermon on the gospel and wanted to demonstrate what the word "sin" means, which is "missing the mark." So I recruited two volunteers who are expert marksmen bowhunters.

We set up a full-size archery target on one end of the stage, and they stood about thirty feet away and each was to shoot an arrow into the target, purposely missing the bulls-eye in dead center. The object was that anything short of dead center was a "miss," a sin ... and that we could not consistently be perfect all the time.

I shared my concern about them missing the entire target, and they assured me that their greatest challenge was to miss dead center.

So, with over a thousand people watching, along with a drum roll, I yelled "Fire!"

The arrow missed the entire target and went through the curtain and shattered on the block wall behind it.

My comeback was that some misses/sins are just bigger than others.

Stay TUNed ... Updates To CoMe

When providing a construction update concerning the new Nursing Mothers' room, our Executive Pastor closed his remarks by saying, "We'll keep you abreast of the progress!"

OFF ON the WroNg Foot

When I was 18 years old and sitting in a Sunday School class, I noticed about halfway through the class that my feet were a little uncomfortable.

When I looked down, I realized my shoes were on the wrong feet!

 Lose Something?

A friend of mine was being baptised and her hairpiece came off when she was immersed.

The preacher just skimmed it off the water, wrung it out and handed it to my red-faced friend, as if nothing was wrong. The whole church burst out laughing during what was supposed to be a very serious and somber moment.

HebreW BiBLe

When my twins were 5 or 6 (they are now 37) our pastor always had a time for the children in the worship service.

One Sunday he explained how in Biblical times, the Hebrew language was what the people spoke and wrote, and showed them some Hebrew writings.

Our daughter got very excited and said she had a Hebrew Bible at home; the pastor asked her to bring it to show to him.

The next Sunday she did just that. As we approached the pastor to say good morning, she brought out a book without a cover that she had found in our garage closet.

As she showed the book to the pastor, we all realized her "Hebrew Bible" was my old shorthand book from college.

WiNdoW DreSSiNg

My 5-year-old son was asking me to draw pictures from the stained glass windows in church.

Not being a good artist, I was not pleasing him as he complained rather loudly, and each time I asked him to whisper.

After I failed at drawing a rooster, he said in a loud voice, "That's not a rooster!" I wanted to crawl in a hole, but left church with him as he yelled, "No, Mommy, no!"

It wasn't funny at the time, but his daughters have asked me to tell that story many times about their dad and we all have a good laugh.

SurgicaL MiSHaP

This happened about fifty years
ago at a church in Arkansas.

During a Sunday evening
service, the hymns had been
sung and now it was time for
prayer requests.

A middle-aged woman stood to
her feet and said, "I would like
for you to pray for
Brother Smith.

"You know he hasn't been
the same since he had that
prostitute surgery."

INKy WaLKS tHe AiSLe

My daddy was a pastor of a small church in Central Louisiana. We lived next door in the church parsonage.

We had several pets, and one was a black cat named Inky.

One Sunday morning we were standing and singing the invitation hymn. No one came forward, but Dad extended the invitation for one more verse.

Suddenly people all over the sanctuary began covering their giggles. I strained to see what was going on, and saw Inky walking down the aisle straight toward my Dad.

She curled herself around my Dad's leg and mewed loudly.

My brothers and I were very young, but the one memory we never forgot as we grew older was the Sunday the cat got saved!

Tall Tale

Our church found a pastor during the summer after a lengthy search process.

Only two ministers remained at our church when the new pastor arrived. One of these left for a mission endeavor that fall, once again leaving us with two ministers. In the early spring, an education minister was found. Very quickly, the pastor pointed out that he was a little intimidated because he was the shortest one on the ministerial staff. Though the pastor was about 6 ft. 2 in. tall, the other two ministers were taller than he was.

In May, we called another minister to the staff who was also much taller than the pastor. One Sunday morning after the sermon, the pastor was making announcements before closing the service.

Suddenly, the music to the song *"Short People"* began playing. From the back of the auditorium came one of the ministers carrying a piece of wood.

I believe another minister came up from the side aisle with another piece. When they got up on the platform, we could tell that they were carrying stilts.

Everyone in the congregation was laughing and clapping!

The pastor pretended to try to get up on the stilts, but thought better of it. He was laughing as much as the rest of us.

I don't believe I have ever seen anything as funny as that in any other service at this church.

Hospital Bed

A church member had been in the hospital and was ready to go home, but he needed a hospital bed at home.

The pastor made an announcement about the need for a hospital bed in the Sunday morning service.

Mrs. Smith raised her hand and announced that she had a hospital bed the man could use.

The pastor replied "I'll get with you on that bed after the service, Mrs. Smith."

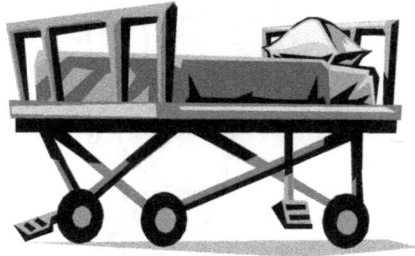

Wardrobe Malfunction

One Sunday while wearing a choir robe
I realized the zipper on my dress was
pulled down under my robe.

Wanting to be discreet, I decided to wait
until I had taken my robe off before I
fixed the zipper.

I didn't want anyone to see, so I backed
up against what I thought was a wall
while I worked the zipper up, hoping
no one would notice.

I didn't realize that the wall wasn't a
wall, it was a window that faced the busy
street at the front of the church!

Littlest Angel

As a longtime pre-school Sunday School teacher,
I have heard many interesting tales from the 4 and
5-year-old set; however, every once in a while I am
still surprised.

As a pre-school teacher, I believe that no age is
too young to begin to hear the story of the Gospel.
Easter is always a great opportunity to share the
story of a Saviour who loved us enough to die on the
cross and then rise again.

This particular Easter was not really any different
than most. I started sharing the story of the cross
(not being too graphic for these 5-year-olds) and
how we all needed a Saviour to take the punishment
for the "wrong things" we had all done.

I watched the wide-eyed excitement as I told about
the women at the empty tomb. As I closed my
lesson, I asked the question, "Aren't you glad that
Jesus was willing to die to take care of all the bad
things we have done?"

At that point, one little boy cocked his head and
said, "Not me, I've never done anything wrong!"

Be Still and Know

Our precocious young daughter was in Sunday School when the teacher asked everyone to sit down for story time.

She didn't want to sit, so she continued to play. Finally, the teacher called her by name and asked her in front of all the other children to come sit down.

She pulled a chair across the floor to sit in, and when she did, said to the teacher, "'Dis be OK?"

The teacher tried her best to cover her mirth at hearing such a young child ask such an adult question.

ALL Creatures Great & SMALL

As very young children are apt to do, our daughter never missed a thing whenever we went to church.

After church for several weeks, we were puzzled when she mentioned the name of someone we couldn't quite get.

We had absolutely no idea who she was referring to.

Finally we made out that she was saying ... "the Creature."

It was not too long before we figured out that she was talking about the "Preacher"!

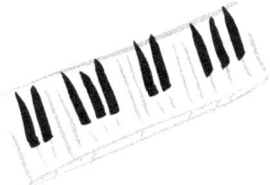

Keyboard Chatter

While my husband served as a pastor in a church in eastern Montana, we had an organist who was extremely talented.

Despite her talent, she had a downright cranky demeanor. We all loved "Clara" (not her real name), but the truth is the truth!

One Sunday morning after a beautifully-played offertory, my husband got to the pulpit to preach, and he wanted to thank "Clara" for her beautifully-played song.

He meant to thank her for "tickling the ivories," … however, he ended up thanking her for "*tinkling* on the ivories."

For the first time in Clara's life she was rendered speechless.

The congregation looked at Clara, then looked at my husband, and then cracked up uncontrollably!

"SIN" OF OMISSION

Our church was hosting the annual carnival for our children's ministry. We needed quite a number of volunteers who would be willing to take a 45-minute shift at various events.

So our secretary meant to put this notice in the bulletin: "We are looking for willing workers to volunteer to take a 45-minute shift at one of our carnival events. Please call the church office if you are willing to help."

That's what she *meant* to write, but she made a typo on the word "shift," leaving out the letter "F".

You can imagine the embarrassment and laughter when this error was discovered on Sunday morning.

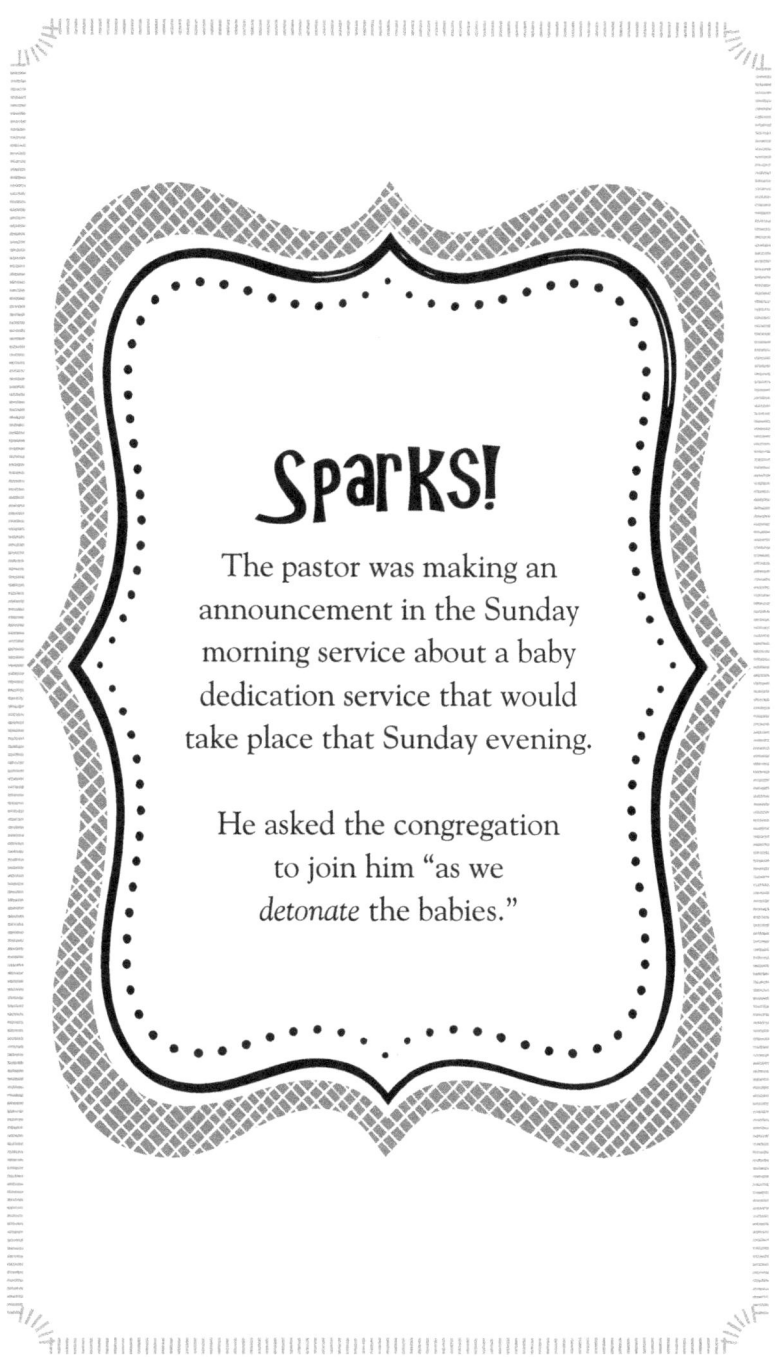

Sparks!

The pastor was making an announcement in the Sunday morning service about a baby dedication service that would take place that Sunday evening.

He asked the congregation to join him "as we *detonate* the babies."

Give Me A "J"!

One Sunday morning the children's choir sang the special music.

They were lined up across the stage and one little girl had been chosen to give a memory verse before they started singing. She was probably 7 or 8, not more than that.

She stepped up to the microphone, put her hands on her hips, and yelled, "OK! John 3:16!"

Then she proceeded to quote the verse.

I kept looking for the rest of the cheerleaders to appear and make a pyramid.

Still, Small Voice

When our children were very young, my husband and I sang in the choir in a little country church in Oklahoma. I directed the choir and hubby sang tenor. Well-meaning church people watched the kids while the choir sang and I led morning worship.

One Sunday while I directed, I saw the people in the back row shuffle around and then backwards and forwards movements like you might see at a theatre when someone needs to leave to go to, well, where ever they feel they need to go to!

During this particular song, no one seemed concerned and no one skipped a beat, no notes were off-key. Suddenly, I hear above a rousing chorus of "Jesus Saves," "I need my comb! Daddy, I need my comb!" and up pops my littlest daughter in her daddy's arms, insistent and squirming.

Now, I hear a slight, tiny commotion, and amid giggles, he hands her his comb and she combs her hair, singing at the top of her little 3-year-old lungs. Then she hopped down and threaded her way back through the tenors and basses to where her handlers were desperately trying to grab her and take her back to the pew.

In a little back-country church, it was cute.

That summer during Vacation Bible School, she pulled the same trick.

Cute?

Not when she shouts, "I gotta poop!" in the middle of a class performance during Parents' Night!

AboUt tHe AUtHor

Sheila Fredrickson has been a book-lover since childhood, when she could nearly always be spotted with a book in her hand. Her earliest recollections of her favorite reads are *Nancy Drew Mysteries*, the *Beezus and Ramona* books by Beverly Cleary, and *Cherry Ames Mysteries*.

Born and raised in Austin, Texas, the school, church and public libraries were a constant source of fun as she discovered the classics, as well as more contemporary inspiration through creative works like *A Wrinkle In Time* by author Madeline L'Engle.

In addition to reading, she began playing the piano at the age of 5 and loved creative projects of all kinds.

Encouraged by wonderful parents, her only limits were in her own mind.

Photo by Melissa Davis

Reading led to writing, and learning to type, but she also enjoyed music, art, journalism and literary activities in junior high, high school and college.

In addition to school activities, her growing up years were spent in church choirs and other church youth activities, and she was at church just about every time the doors were open.

After graduating from Mary Hardin-Baylor College in Belton, TX (now the University of Mary Hardin-Baylor) , she married her college sweetheart, Buddy, and they served Southern Baptist churches in Texas before settling down in Fort Worth to raise their children.

Faith and church life have been the source of many of her best friendships and great memories of the past.

For the last 25 years she has spent her work life as a nonprofit communications professional while doing occasional freelance graphic and web design projects.

She began working with self-publishing authors in 2005.

In 2008, she published a marketing title by business legend Ted Nicholas.

Sheila lives with her husband Buddy, and their cats, in Fort Worth, TX. They have two grown children.

Publish Your Family History or Genealogy Book!

Do you want to publish a family history, years of painstaking genealogical research, or an untold historical story?

It might be a family history going back many generations with information about your great-great-grandparents and other members of your family, complete with photos and family tree information.

It might be a book documenting an actual personal experience, or the experience of someone else in your family; or it might even be a book of reference material resulting from years of research, with names, dates, and family information.

No matter what the focus of your book is, it would be our pleasure to help you get it into print.

We also have, on staff, a certified genealogist available to us as an in-house project consultant.

www.GenealogyBookPublisher.com

Visit **www.OnlyInChurch.com**
to send your funny stories for
Only In Church, Volume II.